Scattered Branches

poems by

Marsha Lewis

Finishing Line Press
Georgetown, Kentucky

Scattered Branches

ACKNOWLEDGMENTS

Grateful acknowledgment is made to the following publications in which
poems from this collection have appeared:

Panoplyzine: "The Depth of Water"
Apricity Magazine: "Scenes from a Lonely Thanksgiving"
Gyroscope: "Ethel in Red"
Black Fox Literary Magazine: "Ebbing"
Lily Poetry Review: "Bread and Butter"
Sepia Quarterly: "A Short History of Portraiture on MacEachen Blvd," "In
Winter"

Publisher: Leah Huete de Maines
Editor: Christen Kincaid
Cover Art: Marsha Lewis
Author Photo: Marsha Lewis
Cover Design: Elizabeth Maines McCleavy

Order online: www.finishinglinepress.com
also available on amazon.com

Author inquiries and mail orders:
Finishing Line Press
PO Box 1626
Georgetown, Kentucky 40324
USA

Contents

Endless Horizon

Purple motel on the edge
of Florida, on the balcony

above a flat state,
across long lines of concrete

you lay bare a highway
dotted with pizza parlors

and blue pools, alligators
in the bushes. I was born

into an endless horizon
matted with sweat,

eternity set out flat
to the horizon, curveless.

There was no hiding place in the sand
or the gravel. Warnings of reptiles

wherever a cool pond lapped.
Lilac-painted buildings

peeling and bleached. I crack
open the broken doorway,

stretch into vacancy and see
the glory of an unmarred sunset

where streetlights flicker
and waver in the heat.

Along the Myakka

The trunks of swamp cypress are
thick here, inward of the sandy beach
where I had growth-spurts and dreamt of
scaling palm trees to the tops of their swaying fronds.

Florida's edges, touristed and wide,
glitter with sand, flash against the deep
shade of mangroves. Glassy-eyed gators
peer from the river, smirking.

Into this dark backyard, I dipped
only a toe. Among dogfennel &
drooping bulrush, fringed the verges
of canals canopied with the long gray
curls of Spanish moss
while dad reported sightings
of Swamp Thing dripping with algae,

armadillos with their peculiar snouts,
their shy armor, burrowing out of sight.
I never spied one, only heard rumors
of a crossing a few feet ahead,
a shout from a further hiker,
shaken palmetto. But I've sensed

proximity to poisonous snakes,
the presence of the prehistoric
in molasses-slow heat,
a smoldering mythology of the real.
I've seen the dark, hungry suck of the mud
as it takes back my footfall.

The possums creep into suburbia.
They look up with flash-lit eyes
and rattle our trash cans.

The Depth of Water

After dusk, we would drive along the
harbor, my father and me
in the dark yawn of gulf
beyond Siesta Village suburbs
painted ostentatious shades
of coral, subdued by moon.
I hung smudged feet
out the window, cut my teeth
on heat and Vietnam stories
softened by vanilla soft-serve cones
from a drive-through window.

Old men peered from the bait shop;
lighted, drunken yachts bobbed by.
He spoke to the night,
rolled down the window,
at peace with the stench of sea
life washed ashore.

Atop the water there is smoothness before
the fish, pierced, is lifted up.
And there are always a few
rainbow trout jumping,
bright and violet,
wet with sharp lace,
but he spoke of long-gone things,
oblivious to the shimmering fish
in front of him.

Saint of Grapefruit

My mother made pies out of grapefruit,
turned bitter citrus into cinnamon-rich
pastry baked up like some Floridian apple.
But juicier, richer, and the rest that ripened,
that fell to the ground, she set out for strangers
on the sidewalk or froze for summer when
we cracked them open and ate the sour, biting slush.
Even the rinds were worth saving

from a tree that we climbed and crashed through,
fell from, threw fruit from, ambushing
neighborhood boys. Soothed by
our own nurse, coming home in scrubs
after a long, fluorescent-lit night
to clean skinned knees, to become a teacher,
to set up a yard-sale blackboard and scribble
in white chalk for the only two students.

We were given violins pretty as cookie-cutters
with their slender necks and wide scrolls,
their carved-out hollows. We picked at strings
'til the shapes on the page turned into language
and we learned their moods—andante, allegro, and so forth.
Sailing into Beethoven with growing angst
while the angrier music she couldn't keep us from
swirled in through windows. A woman
raised for stillness stepping to it deftly.

Mennonite priestess, silent theologian.
Her religion as a refuge where all the love
that ever lit burns warm. As orange
as the orbs on the orange tree.

In Which My Father's Memories Become My Own

There were ghosts in the attic.

In my aunt's story, she speaks
of whispered voices, the screen door
banging faintly through the night.
A scrap of fabric found there
in the morning. Some chance happening,
some brief encounter with grandpa,
lost in his dark war wounds.
All was ghost, and no one spoke
of his time in a stone-gray institution.

Phantoms went round & round. They haunted
orphaned boys who pretended to be warriors
when they were shaken, driven
straight to boot camp at seventeen.

Before then, playing checkers in an empty kitchen
to ignore the stomach's gnaw, rooting through shelves.
I remember like this morning the bare fridge.
Mustard sandwiches for motherless tongues.

And all the while, that neighbor boy
on the porch, flaunting his grape soda-pop.

A Brief History of Portraiture on MacEachen Blvd

I felt nothing in the room where spirits
should have risen from the carpet, where hymns
weren't sung. The oxygen tank hummed
and I made lemon cake, his final request.
He could have fallen in surprise at this from a daughter.

Me at ten, throwing away Marlboros by the pack,
hauling the little tv from his room because I hated the sad glow.
How angry he was at being saved from cancer,
at my tiny and furious persistence.
He was a master of pictures, his one art;
sketching expressions, detailing intricate faces
then crumpling them in frustration.
In the garbage, masterpieces trashed.

My father used to draw me in charcoal,
and rendered there I saw myself unfinished:
the portrait of me had no mouth.

In the end, I bring my voice,
but all he asks for is a soda.
Ice-cold and sugared, please,
resigned lungs hoarse for relief.

Recital of Falsehoods Accompanied by Strings

It was a Saturday. The wind blew.
I touched the glass and looked out
onto an empty street for signs
of a car. Every weekend, the chill
picks up its pace, the television fizzles into static,
and the bicycles left lying
somewhere rust.

That was a day full of panic
in a movement-less world.
A sting of winter, though the calendars promised
almost May. Nothing on tv, just waiting
to leave. With rosin and polished bow.

I watched my sister, her dark hair
blown slightly frizzy by the breeze.
She wore a red scarf in the driveway
as daylight disappeared, wondering
who would take us to the hall of violins.

It was just another day,
the beginning of absence
and sharp things
lying everywhere
beneath soft cotton.

Wind that turned and turned.

The trust of twelve winters crumbled
behind me, a sky full of ash.

Youth Group

In the halls, movies of summer.

They ordered pizzas with meat
I didn't touch: dead pig on cheese,
splotched with grease, the boys loud.

Boys with rude movements
in lieu of words, trained to talk
of holiness when the minister entered,

to tangle theology with football
metaphors. At twelve, I towered
above like an errant question mark.

I spent the weekend in a room
of teenaged females who swapped
brand-name bags and knew
how to brush each other's hair.

Mine spiraled like the snakes of Medusa,
hair like fire ants in a field of corn silk.
I kept mine safe from fingers,
a wall as thick as the Bible around me.
Flashlights burst in corridors, the sound
of jokes far away. Heat prickled
beneath the skin of *anawim.**

We were beginning to bleed
into America. When light broke
like a strange beacon beyond

that white room, it woke no one
and barely stirred the sound sleepers.

*Anawim is a Hebrew word meaning the poor and the oppressed.

Ethel in Red

Instead of the muted beige she
is modest in, a brash-colored cloth
flutters. Licks the horizon line
like flame, flies out beyond her.

Will that be her afterlife,
a lush flamenco watercolor,
for years of sewing rips
and threading unspoken anger
through the needle?
What is the reward for tight-lipped prudence
while frustration rifles its way
into your joints?

I would give her fabric
the color of madness and watch
what it becomes under her thumb ,
in her skill see it turn
into a skirt that carries fire-

wood, thread, supper
casseroles and the emotions
of the ministers around her
in hidden pockets. Then sweep it into

a glorious whirl of blur
that centers her, its calm eye,
til she is ready to reveal
herself as crimson, furious,
desirous of full-throated rage.

Praxis

After a wakeful night when the trees did not walk,
and still, the sky didn't turn blood-red,
there was Easter. Rising light, spring, swelled
and loomed. I left dad with his
apocalyptic prophecies, smaller in the
morning air. Went with mint and
lamb to worship. My mother's mothers
wore lace prayer caps and harmonized.

I had, in my flowered dress, a mistrust
of congregating masses, inherited
the wariness of a veteran, his solitary guard.
I learned to question the sermons of men
behind podiums, but I wanted to follow
those women with quiet necks and covered heads
into wherever they went to.

How I wanted belonging which the
skepticism of everything
kept me from. How I wanted
their easy shunning of falsehoods,
defenselessness of deep knowing;
No need for shields or arrows.

Theological arguments exhausted breath
and worried the children. Uncles in their
clenched-fist armchairs with their
varying diagrams of hell.

Grandma kneaded potato rolls,
pressed her nails into the sides
of risen proof. Multiplied them
into baskets, light and feathery
softness melting away
the hunger of neighbors.

Bread and Butter

Sweet cream of fontina,
ricotta, and mozzarella
in a deep red sauce.
I eat the three cheeses
in their butter-yellow pillows
of flour: oh flour, sacred and ancient,
now maligned for the long strands
which weave it together,
which make it malleable;
flour that calmed my belly
ache with each saltine
of fluted edges and dry calm,
toast that I smothered with jam.

It is not the sweet cream or the
wheat that wrecks us now.
Wagers of war rain down their wares
upon our bread and butter:
malathion, name like a plague or a pharaoh,
rivering through wet rice,
glyphosate ground into our grain.

I search for amaranth, einkorn, triticale,
spelt that grew before my grandmother's days;
weigh the consequences of almond milk,
the ruin of bees and well-being of heifers,

as world-over, workers in old towns
with worn hands
twist dough into challah,
smash it into tortillas
and churn fat-full milk from the cow
into a stick of spun gold.

In A Maze of Mottled Fruit

It began with apples.

Within them, between the leaves,
a wet light. The limbs form a tight circle.
To pursue that luminescence
would mean to entangle one's own
limbs in the branches.
I wandered from redwood to redwood
in the foothills of the Sierras,
in gold mining country, until I came to
this patch of pear and apple.

They were unrecognizable to me
in the stretched-out shadows of the day,
these golden amber ovals in the grove.

I should say I found a place to rest at last
and it was well with me, for I had eaten
my fill of sweetness, yet I hungered.
Took a bite from each piece of fruit,
demanded backtalk from the mute sky.
The long evening sat in the leaves
and looked back at me.

Wind shook through branches, hours
past dinnertime, into the light left,
getting late. It sounded like laughter

to the forlorn red-apple-eater
lying in a splotch of warmth
scattered with cores.

For Laura, When You Need the Water

Wake to cicadas.

Honey-colored, busted-out skulls
crunch in every footstep,

a humming song lush enough to
deafen in the halls of trees, of conifers.

Leave the understory of bitterbrush
with its pungent leaves and solitary yellow

flowers behind, as it reclaims mined land.
Leave yesterday's bitter story in its year.

Beyond, a tea-colored lake sifts gold
through cones and tannins.

You could take out the abandoned canoe,
red and rusted, press oars through sediment

to where waves ripple, where they carry
you into trembling refraction, into rays

of wide open exposure to the sun.
How it uncovers everything, pure afternoon.

Shadows come alive in such brightness—
Startling shadows from foothill pines.

And your own, as you stir the surface,
peer over the edge, and see

your self as a clear lake
beneath blue-green algae.

Drought And Other Things No One Noticed

Even now, birds dive for ripe grapes
with sugar-stunned tongues. Squawk angrily
at how I take the ripest ones, unstung
by yellow-and-black insects buzzing. I know nothing
of these winged thieves—their name or
need or where they go, where they fly to.

Only that the heat this year has challenged
even the sturdiest of shrubs. That the dry ground
drives ants into battle. Beneath us, little behemoths
brandish their spears and venture out
to wage war for water. I'll go where
I remember a pond, where cows lift their mouths
and consider radio waves in languid wind.

Brown-eyed Susans droop in the driest
soil of ages, nodding off to curl into death
and earth. Grass like cornflakes. Thirst
(but not in our throats). Even now,
streams rush from silver faucets at my whim.

I exile heaps of shining garbage
to a rusted truck at dawn
and worry little of the ocean.
Even now, cars fly by with their
tops down, furiously shiny,
enjoying the last days of oil.

Tricks of Light

Against six o'clock, these gold dancers
tremble, once leaves. Cloud-jagged
darkness comes in slow but early.
Hold the light, we cry—wait! a little longer—
but for what? We made so little of it
these past months, rushed inside walls
away from warmth. Yet still its loss is dreadful,
now that dusk crawls across low roads
with hands painted in henna.

Fall's strange lantern transforms
even the edges of dull homes—
castles now, purpled,
abandoned penitentiaries,
cathedrals jabbing shadows through
an ochre, stained-glass Christ.

I shift and change in angles
as an hour moves: glow, worry,
grow golden-red and soften
or turn into stone a little
more as we all turn
around and around the late axis.

Night Blooms

Trumpet flowers open, shaped
like the sound of the moon

through a gramophone,
dull lull of a womb,

the edges of petals expanding
as earth pulls up her blanket.

Datura re-seeds itself, poison-
ous, violet-edged, for next year,

takes over the empty white
ballroom of longing

on the moon-lit lawn.
Jealousy blooms intrusive.

What is envy but loneliness,
what is an invasive species

but a root reaching forward,
a restless ecosystem

sowing its own survival.
The moon has her mustache

of black cloud tonight, cosmic
shifts in a hormonal tide.

O shape of ache.
Opaque circles move across the sky,

Many moons, many ovaries
weep and empty.

Off the Grid

We live simply among trees
built for giants, sequoias in red clay
beneath the Sierras. Our neighbors collect war machines,
drive auctioned-off tanks along the wooded road,
or practice reiki in their commune: o the outliers
this unbridled landscape beckons in.

Isolation winds its way to the cabin.

I make bagels to lengthen
the already-long weeks of absence
and learn of yeast, of heat,
how much kills the frothing sponge,
how much feeds it.

I twist and fit into the silence.

Sometimes I walk to visit
a woman in a trailer down the lane
whose worsening aloneness drives her
to scenes of excess, making mobiles of glass shards
which spin from every tree limb, tending succulents
in her cactus garden. Pruning away
at the ancient desire to be loved
as though more practice could cure it.
Her almond-eyed, elf-like cat goes hunting alone,
as hungry for wildness as we are.

The land is thick with manzanita,
little trees with beautifully contorted branches.
Manzanita wood makes fire so hot it will melt the woodstove,
and we are warned of this. Together, look
for fallen logs to light that will bring us
warmth without burning us up.

Chop Wood, Carry Water*

Dawn rises through leaves of spinach,
where little seedlings shiver.
Hands gather lettuce, then slice
green-wet herbs, sharp-scented.

I unearth beets with their maudlin
plum-dark hearts, beets as deep
purple as the memories in bruised land,
a wealth of rich rebirth raked on
to return what was taken.

This is how I share in the world's
long history, with those made to dig
and lift what fed lavish kings.
Thorns of thistle prick my privileged

fingers. I do not want to break the earth
with long tools of wood and metal,
nor myself, but to turn lightly towards the air
our lungs, and breathe in
what clover can do for us both.

The wide land beckons,
calls with its scurrying kildeer
to move through fields
that exhaust the laborious body
into a sheen, then a calm.

Under shadow & sweat drop,
earth, that great cavern, opens
and offers up potatoes, growing
in their labyrinth for months.
Red and gold and dust-covered,
rolling just out of reach.

I brush off soil in clods.
I am busy with nothing but sustenance.
Earth. worms. rocks. roots.
And buckets of carrots to carry,
and heads of green cabbage to wash.

*"Chop Wood, Carry Water," which is a zen proverb. "The origin is a verse
by the late eighth-century Chinese poet Layman Pang, who declared that his
"supernatural power and marvelous activity" was "drawing water and carrying
firewood."

Night Scene in Homestead, Florida

In the barn, a hot Florida shelter along the edge of Miami
where acres of flat tomato farms stretch on for miles,
we peel oranges and talk of hurricanes. We live for now
in a tucked-away oasis of limes, having chosen

the road lined with sugarcane and fire-ant-hilled sand,
to sleep by cobwebs and boxes in the merciless humidity
for a month or two, alongside Pedro, steady and year-round,
mired in silence. He polished eggs at the stone foot
of the stairs, our only shared language a hum.

My nightly entertainment was the drama of spider vs. moth.
A luna moth, large as a bird, careened through, drawn to
my light: that foreboding lone hanging lightbulb
ever-present in nightmares but here warm, with dust netting

and lost wing of insect, a family of fluttering bugs agog,
glazed-eyed for its yellow above softening papayas.
Nearby, Sadie in her hammock, blue-eyed and pushing forty,
swings herself to sleep in the avocado grove.

Mary and the Crows

A black-feathered gathering
rustles in the oak. Mary watches them
with her worn brown jacket's
hood half over her forehead,
fiddles with knife & zipper, ragged hem,
gleaning insights on the pattern
of the lone feathered scout's November
stalking as we gather the year's last greens.

"It's a decoy," she tells me, "a scout,"
each singular yellow eye following
the truck's muddy path to the patch
of spinach, flowering yellow mustards,
and jagged, tall leaves of mizuna.

Does it watch us watching,
weighing its macabre image of rustling
purple against its ordinariness,
and wonder the same of us?
Does it tell the others tales of us as a threat
or a riddle, a folk story, a myth?

Such whip-smart birds
who collect forgotten glimmer
and scraps of shine,
who hold funerals for one another,
leave mementos in a circle,
metal tabs threaded on pine twigs.

And are they crows or ravens anyway,
these creatures of indigo iridescence
with their neckless heads turning nearly in circles,
their relentless stares?

After September

At the end of a sun-washed season,
we walked the edges of fields picked over,
tangled with mallow and thistle, ·
row upon row of rich greens
devastated by the mandibles of bugs.
Chive flowers exploded purple and burst
open, feathery as hydrangeas,
made pungent the long, drawn-out summer.
A few onions lying scattered
from last month's harvest, pulled
on days wilted by July's thick air,
heavy soil clinging to their bulbs.

In the furthest plot, we dug up sweet potatoes,
shovels pulling pain sharp through
a back bent for hours, and sought to
preserve the smooth skin of tubers.
Working on a land that wasn't ours, each with a history
that stores it soreness in different places,
remembered by muscles
woken loud. We were women
who proved our worth with blisters.
 A sisterhood of mud boots
and clay, we would mold it into loam,
feed each other feasts we grew from seed.

I would seek the virtues and remedies
of weeds, of burdock for raw
aching joints, bring them in
in fat bunches wet with mud,
lay out roots of dandelion for drying,
stinging nettle leaves and chickweed,
then abandon the experiment,
a hill of ragged leaves
untidying the kitchen.

Someone would make a soup for dinner.
Root through the pile of obscure vegetables—
parsnip, romanesco—cluttering our table and leave
a bright red, bleeding tomato sliced open.

Scenes From a Lonely Thanksgiving

Today I have loved a stray cat walking by,
its small shape against tree trunk, the pause
to smell what was lost there
before it, to inhale the traces.
And a woman with a bottle of cabernet
hurrying through the grocery,
a blur of rush in ill-fitting velvet
vexed by time.

Some dress like this, in shaky heels,
to adorn a gathering of twinkling silver
and tinny, light conversation.
Others grab their yearly sandwich
from the gas station deli, stuffed
with sour mashed berries
and pale meat,
wet bread on bread.

It is a contest of community,
this homage to ancient theft
and artifice of friendship.
It is a leaving-out or inviting-in:
a marker for how alone you are.

Once I burnished my great aunt's
ruby red goblets
in a room full of noise and stories.

Now I bake blind pie crusts,
walk empty parks and bridges,
nod to the man with deep-set eyes
on the periphery of the Perkiomen,
leave out a plate for feral creatures.

Ocean City, October

The damp weather
hangs between hot & cold—
salt-soaked papers in late day
fading, gritty sand sharp with pebbles
and disintegrating shells,

each nerve ending illuminated
in the red sun of Ocean City,
half empty this late in the year.

We walked the boardwalk
last night, past arcades shut down
'til next summer.
You love it vacant,
stone-cold and nearly dead.

In an abandoned amusement park,
we sat side by side on the Jolly Roger,
an empty rollercoaster we trespassed,
its thrills rusting shut in sea air.

"I'm just waiting," you said, "for this
to be over, so I can sleep."
Faded plastic clowns gaped at us,
open mouths pink as a wound.

Seagulls circled like white Kleenex
in strange late patterns,
droves and droves of them
in the dark.

They are still there, perhaps,
flashing above the Atlantic,
waving their white kerchiefs
like I am, at the edge of the pier.

Night Drive

In thickening woods, the headlights
throw sharp shapes down
a drive of bright tunnels before us,
gravelly turns, dark growling blips
on the dashboard before the radio goes.

In the headlights, a red-eyed animal
soft with the wetness of its last feed.
The scent of it comes in your window.

Late August, nine o'clock, and I understand
the hunger of a coyote for
warmth in another body, in one I have
chased and wearied myself over.

I understand, too, the deer.

We sit in silence as the engine dies.
Wait in the pitch-black for rescue.

Acts of God

In scenes of fire, collapse, & flood
I've not imagined myself.
At eight, I holed up in the closet,
windows rattling in a hurricane.
Knees to chin, I waited,
listening for devastation
as each successive summer,
another storm passed without remark:
for me, lightning was a flash of theatre,
the hot danger fluttering too far for harm.

I knew nothing of high waters,
stranded pets and flooded bedrooms in Louisiana.
I visited and ate crawdads, thrilled at the long canals where gators lurk
and creole accents that curled words into new language.
The orchid-bright clang of the trolley
took me to Bourbon Street and riverboats.

But keep your focus, for here is the work:
the deck of the mobile home
that collapsed, the ramp for a wheelchair.
We repair it well, build walls worthy of admiration,
construct a wooden ramp sturdy as our work ethic,
our pride, then turn our wheels
out of gravel lots, away from hot metal
FEMA trailers as far as the eye can see.

I would sit in the corner of that dim trailer,
watch the creases in her ancient forehead
change shape as she spoke and listen
while the drills squealed and the hammers thudded
outside, repairing what can be repaired.

Nun In Ecstasy

St Catherine's head in a glass jar,
her little skull a cathedral.
In Cornaro, the statue of
Teresa's parted mouth.
She shushes us from the deep hush
of her emaciated cloister.
Hears the far-off hum of a quiet God.

The saint I read of lived on herbs.
I want to be painted with ashes,
like her. To fast. The distractions
of my body leaving me briefly
empty, til even a taste of stale
bread brings a flood of reverence.

And then to feast, to feed figs
to the mouth of hunger, grant sleep
to restless minds and worn-out joints.
A slice of iced cake for every saint.

I've not walked til my ankles swelled
on a dusty road, but long to touch holiness'
ragged cloak. To gather crumbs with Syrophoenician
women on the edges of what is forgotten and true.

Let the faithful preserve our ghosts.
We know what to build upon
and what to let decompose,
the difference between skeleton and flesh.

Ebbing

Pale Ovaltine in clean jars,
an ivory soap smell, little cracked
glasses along the ledge.

As she declined, I scrubbed feathery, fuzz-green mildew
from the birdbath. A cardinal visited the feeder
and she knew it to be her husband
flitting there, red-feathered.

She grew softer as she ripened into even quieter wisdom,
wrote in tinier, tinier blue ink on thank-you cards.

She will lift a skillet in the kitchen some afternoon
and stand still while listening to a thing unheard before,
then put down her heavy utensils, the old ways
of knowing, for the time when they were needed
is past now. It rings in the ears, a vague tinnitus.

And speaking from this watery new place
to the land-locked, she sounds confused.
You'll hurry on in ramblings to stun the hush, to fill it:
ask questions to keep her grounded, place cups and calendars
near as reminders, but never mind: the concrete cannot keep her here.

She has a rare silken quality
in her sinew; she goes into silvering spaces.

In Winter

I.

Only the dog people emerge in freezing weather.
Hunched beneath hoods, they follow pawprints
of large-jawed mammals who sniff rocks
and lead them across ice-botched cement,
past the place where newspapers land, to urinate on fire
protection, suburbanites' oblivious fenceposts.

Inside, there's a soup maker with her back
to the window, unaware of how many furred
creatures circle the sidewalk tonight,
picking up the scent of roast beef.

II.

The cats look for me now from the cold barn,
hoping for tins of salmon. I began as the water froze
to visit late, after work, entering a doorway
I feared. Past rusted metal rakes, old milk tins,
gnarled tractor implements in a dim flicker
to fill their corner with fresh drink.

Now they know time and weather and wait.
They peer from the doorway
with eyes that glow iridescent,
twitching their white-tipped tails.

III.

Shrinking, wrinkled people stay inside
by the window, wonder where their offspring
went and when the phone will vibrate.

There are little children in their mirrors.

They cover themselves with thick wool.

IV.

Those without homes will find a bus stop
to make the long, concrete benches
of night softer, the ache less alone.
In the city, long lines of hunger turn beneath
such majestic buildings, marvels of architecture,
marvels of marble and steel. Electric lights
waver cobalt and coral over pavement.

Tonight it's so frigid, there's a warning to bring in your pets.
Those sleeping on church steps will waken to frostbite
and the rich will float in pink salt.

V.

Little home with a window
above the highway. Here by
the heater, who could squeeze in?
Haven't I watched the whole world
shudder in its own cold?

I stir my soup-pot of potatoes
and curl beneath a wool blanket,
two orange-glowing candles on the sill.

Travelers pass by this lamp and window.
It's been on the edge
of the interstate for ages, high-hilled.

Old house beneath a yellow moon.

Snowstorm Before the Second Spring

The silence of moved snow when we could touch
meant the cleared roads would bring us to one another
with uncovered mouths.

It's quiet as a chime, how subdued,
each flake falling. The only sound

is the scrape of shovel.
Neighbors stay in, distant;

rabbit tracks zig-zag across the year.
An amaryllis blooms live as a virus.

And it's a deep February, deep,
buried in our own hovels.

In my own chest, an ice storm
muted. I've sunken in a snowbank

and shouted into the
glacial darkness until hollers glowed

to break open this lone hush,
to sing with visible lips again.

Plows keep our pathways open
as we listen to the slow melt.

A drip becomes a river;
little mammals come to drink from it.

When the ice cracks, the animals show.
Soon, a burst purple crocus.

Marsha Lewis was born & raised in South Florida and now lives in the Philadelphia region. Her poems have appeared in *Panoplyzine, Apricity, Red Weather, Gyroscope, Black Fox Literary Review, Lily Poetry Review*, and others. This is her first collection.